A BRIEFE INTRO
duction to the skill of
SONG:

*Concerning the practise, set forth
by William Bathe*
Gentleman.

In which work is set downe X. sundry wayes of 2. parts
in one vpon the plaine song. Also a Table newly added of the comparisons of Cleues, how one followeth
another for the naming of Notes : with other neces-
farie examples, to further the learner.

FABIVS.

*Musica est honestum et iucundum oble ctamen-
tum, liberalibus ingenijs maxime dignum.*

LONDON
Printed by Thomas Este.

William Balfe:
A Briefe Introduction to the Skill of Song.
Facsimile.

First published circa 1587.

Republished Travis & Emery 2008.

Published by
Travis & Emery Music Bookshop
17 Cecil Court, London, WC2N 4EZ, United Kingdom.
(+44) 20 7240 2129
neworders@travis-and-emery.com

Hardback: ISBN10: 1-904331-69-6   ISBN13: 978-1904331-69-8
Paperback: ISBN10: 1-904331-70-X   ISBN13: 978-1904331-70-4

A BRIEFE INTRO
duction to the skill of
SONG:

*Concerning the practise, set forth
by William Bathe*
Gentleman.

In which work is set downe X. sundry wayes of 2. parts
in one vpon the plaine song. Also a Table newly added of the comparisons of Cleues, how one followeth
another for the naming of Notes : with other necef-
farie examples, to further the learner.

FABIVS.

*Musica est honestum et iucundum oblectamen-
tum, liberalibus ingenijs maxime dignum.*

LONDON
Printed by Thomas Este.

To the Reader.

Gnorance as Diuines doe testifie, is one of the plagues put vpon man the creature, for transgressing of the commaundements of God his creatour, from which we are to come, (as the patient from his disease)by degrees. Mans vnderstanding is likened by Aristotle to the eies of the Howlet in the day-light Salomon sayth : Dedi cor meum vt scirem prudentiam, doctrinam, erroresq;, et stultitiam, et agnoui quod in his quoq; est labor et atflictio spiritus.

The same of our ancestours that diligently laboured to bring vs, and in many things brought vs, from ignorance to knowledge, shall neuer be forgotten so long as those things wherein they laboured, be in estimation, and(in mine opinion)so farre forth as we may, we should Imitate the steps of them, for this plague of ignorance is so great, that neither did they, neither shall we finde so much : but that we must leaue sufficient, for our posteritie to be found.

Wherefore seeing sufficiently others to labour and trauell in other Sciences, I thought good to bestow my labour in Musicke, seeing that paines might so much preuaile, as by the fruit of my labour may plainly appeare. I tooke the matter in hand vpon this occasion, though it were far distant from my profession, being desired by a gentleman, to instruct him in song, I gaue him such rules as my Master gaue mee : Yet could I giue him no song so plaine, wherein there chanced not some one thing or other, to which none of those rules could directly leade him. Marking then how in minde, I did know what by rule I could not teach, I perceiued how

To the Reader.

*vnder the shade of rule, I attained to many things by rote,
and how pleasant, speedie and sure it is to runne by rule, I
tooke this labour in hand, and brought it to this passe. Olde
Musitions laid downe for Song, manifold and crabbed,
confuse, tedious rules, as for example: though there be in
all but sixe names, Vt, Re, Mi, Fa, Sol. La. hauing amongst
them an easie order, yet could not they by rule declare, whether of these should bee attributed to euery Note, vnlesse
they had first framed the long ladder or skale of Gam-vt,
to which some added, thinking the ladder too short, some
hewed off a peece, thinking it too long. Then would they
haue the learner be as perfect in comming downe backward, as in going vp forward, least in his practise he should
fall, and breake his neck. Then must he learne, Gam-vt, in
rule, Are, in space, b mi in rule, C faut in space, &c. Then
must he know Gam vt, how many cleues, how many notes.
Are, how many notes, &c. Then must he know b, quadrij,
proper chant and bemul, re in Are, whereby vt in Cfaut,
whereby mi, in Alamire, whereby &c And when all haue
done, after their long circumstances of time, whereby they
should be often driuen to millibi, for Notes standing in di-
uerse places of Gam-vt, haue names that the place where
they stand comprehend not. Touching all the prolixe circumstances, & needlesse difficulties, that they vse, it loathes
me greatly that heere I should write them: & much more
would it grieue the Reader to learne them. Also many
things are vsed in Song, for which they giue no rules at all,
but committed them to dodge at it, harke to it, and harpe
vpon it. Now (Reader) th'effect of my pretended purpose,
and fruit of my finished labor is this, where they gaue pro-*

                                                                lixe

lixe rules, I haue giuen briefe rules, where they gaue vncertaine rules, I haue giuen sure rules, and where they
haue giuen no rules, I haue giuen rules. After all this that
I haue said of their rules, I doe affirme that they deserued
greater commendations aboue mee, for finding out the long
way, then I aboue others for laying down the short way. For
had not they opened the gappe, touching mee, it might very
well hap that I should in no sort enter my selfe, and much
lesse in any sort inuite others : nothing can at the beginning be perfected, and therefore are they to bee holden ex-
cused as the old verse hath :

But ere the Painter can sure his craft attaine,
Much froward facion transformeth hee in vayne,
By rayfing superfluitie, and adding that doth want,
Rude Pictures are made both perfect and pleasant.
For such things by negligence are left vndone,
That by good diligence might be wonne.

There be sufficient, many, and firme prooues had of this
that I say, which may by my rules be done, of which I will
heere put downe some of them, though I get as little by being beleeued, as I should loose by being belyed.

In a moneth and lesse I instructed a child about the age
of eight yeeres, to sing a good number of songs, difficult
crabbed Songs, to sing at the first sight, to be so indifferent
for all parts, alterations, Cleues, flats, and sharpes, that he
could sing a part of that kinde, of which he neuer learned
any song, which child for strangenesse was brought before
the Lord Deputie of Ireland, to be heard sing : for there
were none of his age, though he were longer at it, nor any
of his time, (though he were elder) knowne beefore these

A.iij.   rules

To the Reader.

rules to fing exactly.

There was another, that had before often handled In-
struments, but neuer practifed to fing (for hee could not
name one Note) who hearing of thefe rules, obtayned in
short time, fuch profit by them, that he could fing a difficult
fong of himfelfe, without any Inftructor.

There was another, who by dodging at it, hearkning to
it, & harping vpon it, could neuer be brought to tune sharps
aright, who fo foone as hee heard thefe rules fet downe for
the fame, could tune them fufficiently well. I haue taught
diuerfe others by thefe rules, in leffe then a moneth; what
my felfe by the olde, obtained not in more then two yeeres.
Diuerfe other proofes I might recite, which heere as need-
leffe I doe omit, becaufe the thing will shew it felfe. Diuerfe
haue repented in their age that they were not put to fing in
their youth; but feeing that by thefe rules, a good skill may
be had in a moneth : and the wayes learned in foure or fiue
dayes : none commeth too late to learne, and fpecially if this
faying be true : That no man is fo olde but thinketh he
may liue one yeere longer. As Ariftotle in fetting forth
his predicaments, faw many things requifite to be entreated
off : and yet vnfit to be mixed with his treatife : he therefore made ante predicaments, and poft predicaments : fo I
for the fame caufe (defirous to abolish confufion) haue added to my rules, ante rules, and poft rules. Vale.

The ante rules of Song.

To prepare for naming the Notes.

PRactise to sunder the Vowels and Consonants, distinctly pronouncing them according to the manner of the place.

To prepare for Quantitie.

PRactise to haue the breath long to continue, and the tongue at libertie to runne.

To prepare for Time.

PRactise in striking to keepe a iust proportion of one stroke to another.

To prepare for Tune.

PRactise to haue your voice cleere, which when thou hast done, learne the rules following.

The skill of song doth consist in foure things,
{
Naming.
Quantitie.
Time.
Tune.
}

The

The Scale of Mufick, which is called Gam-vt, contei-
neth 10 rules, and as many fpaces; and is fet downe
in letters and fillables, in which you muft beegin at
the loweft word, Gam-vt, and fo go vpwards to the
end ftill afcending, and learne it perfectly without
booke, to fay it forwards and backewards : to know,
wherein euery key ftandeth, whether in rule or in
fpace : and how many Cliefes, how many Notes is
contayned in euery Key.

Hic. Middeft. Low.

ee	la			1 Note
dd	la	fol		2 Notes
cc	fol	fa		2 Notes
bb	fa	b-mi		2 Notes 2 Cliffes
aa	la	mi	re	3 Notes
g	fol	re	vt	3 Notes
f	fa	Vt		2 Notes
e	la	mi		2 Notes
d	la	fol	re	3 Notes
c	fol	fa	vt	3 Notes
b	fa	b-mi		2 Notes 2 Cliffes
a	la	mi	re	3 Notes
G	fol	re	vt	3 Notes
F	fa	vt		2 Notes
E	la	mi		2 Notes
D	fol	re		2 Notes
C	fa	vt		2 Notes
B	mi			1 Note
A	re			1 Note
Γ	vt			1 Note

For Naming. Cap. primo.

There bee fixe names, Vt, Re, Mi, Fa, Sol, La.
The order of afcention & defcention with them is thus.

Exceptions

Rules of Song.

Exceptions.

Change Vt, into Sol, change -Re, into La, when the
next remouing Note is vnder.

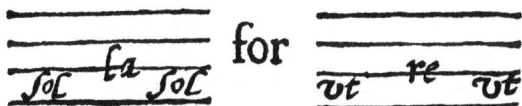

The Cleues whereby we know where the *Vt* ſtandeth
are thus marked as.

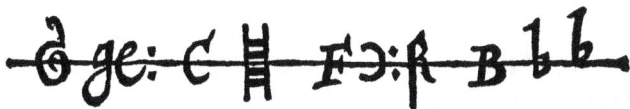

The *G :* cliefe is the mark of the higher *G ſol re vt.*
In the ſcale:& the *C:*clefe of that place called *C ſol fa vt.*
And the *F :* cliefe of *F fa vt* the lower in the ſcale.

Now in this ſort you may finde by the cliefe where e-
uery note ſtandeth : and leaſt there ſhould ſeeme any
difficultie,I will begin from the firſt ſight of the booke,
that all things that doe belong to their knowledge,may
bee the better vnderſtoode. Firſt when a man ſeeth the
booke before him he may ſee certaine rules which goe
along lineally by 5 and 5 which number of 5 is called a
ſet of prickſong(for a ſet of plaineſong hath commonly but 4.rules,) then he may ſee in the firſt of the ſet alwayes one of the foreſayde cleifes vpon ſome rule, and
whatſoeuer note ſtandeth vpon the ſame rule with the
cliefe,is ſaid to be in that place wherof that cleife which

he

he seeth is the marke, and if any note stand in the next
space aboue, it is said to stand in the next place aboue
that place, whereof that cleife is the marke. And so vpward and downeward continually counting from the
close as in this example.

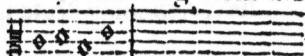

The first note standeth in *C sol fa vt*, because it standeth vpon the same rule with the clief which is the mark
of *C sol fa vt*, the second in *D la sol re*, because *D la sol re*
is next aboue *C sol fa vt* in the scale of *Gam vt*: the third
in *B fa b mi*, because it is in the next place beneath *C sol
fa vt*: the fourth in *E la mi*, because *E la mi* is the next
place saue one to *C sol fa vt*, & the said fourth note standeth in the next place saue one to the cliefe which is the
mark of the place *C sol fa vt*. And so of all other notes:
then in the ende of the set, hee may see a thing thus
marked, which is called a direct, because it is alwayes
put vpon the rule or space wherein the first of the next
set standeth, and doth so direct a man, euen as in bookes
the word that is lowest vpon euery side of the leafe doth
direct a man to the word next following.

The rule of Vt.

The next thing necessary to be knowne for the right
naming of notes, is the place where that note standeth
which is named *Vt*. And as by counting vpward and
downeward from the cliefe it is to bee knowne where
euery note standeth, so it is to be knowne by counting
vpward and downeward from that which is called *Vt*,
what the right name of euery note is: but first let vs set
downe how the place where the *vt* standeth is knowen,

which

which is thus. There be three places, in one of which the
vt muſt alwaies be : that is to ſay, in *G*. which is *Gamut*
and *G ſol re vt*, when there is no flat in *C*, which is *C fa
vt*, *C ſol fa vt*, and *C ſol fa*, when there is a flat in *b mi*,
or *b fa b mi*. In *F* which is *F fa vt*, when there are two
flats, one in *b mi* or *b fa b mi*, the other in *E la mi*, or *E la*.
As for example.

Now the *vt* is in *G*.　Now in *C*.　　Now in *F*.

¶ No b flat, the *(vt)* in **G**. The b flat in b onely, the
(vt) in **C**. The b flat in b and E, the *(vt)* in **F**.

1 　G putteth *Vt* to the ſame place.

2 ⎫
3 ⎬ F. and B. to the next vp, as.
　 ⎭

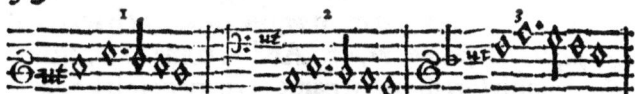

4 　C putteth *Vt* to the fift place vp, and from C down
　　to the fourth. B, taketh place of the reſt.
　 B, is placed laſt to ſhew that it taketh place of the reſt.
5 　If there commeth two, b.b. being a fourth, the vp-
　　per taketh place.
6 　And being a fift, the nether taketh place, as :

7 D. putteth *Vt* to the fift place downe, but it is sel-
dome vsed.

8 If there commeth two b.b. being a second a sunder,
the vpper taketh place, which chanceth very rare.

More shall be sayd of naming in the chapter of tuning.

When you haue in this sort found out the *vt*, you
must vnderstand that euery note that standeth in the
next place aboue it is named *re*, euery note that standeth
in the next place to that is named *mi*, in the next to that
fa, then *sol*, then *la*, then *fa*, ascending vp alwaies orderly,
counting the rules, and spaces: then next aboue that a-
gaine is *vt* : for you shall finde that place, which is the
eight place from that wherein your other *vt* stood, to
begin with the same letter : So that if the rules & spaces were infinite, you might in this manner giue euery
note his right name : and as you did count vpward *Vt*,
re, *mi*, *fa*, *sol*, *la*, *fa*, and so come againe to *vt* : so must
you come downeward from *vt*, the same way backward,
by *fa*, *la*, *sol*, *fa*, *mi*, *re*, *vt*. And so come to *fa*, againe.
And in this sort the right name of euery note is knowne.
Two things from these rules are excepted, the one is,
that euery *re*, should be named *la*, when you ascend to
it, or descend from it : and that euery *vt*, should bee named *sol*, which two things are vsed *euphoniæ gratia*, and
yet this name of *vt*, is most proper to the base or lowest
part in the first place.

Obiection against the latter exception.

In the latter exception it is said, that *vt* should be alwaies changed into *sol*, therefore seeing it is neuer vsed,

it is in vaine placed in all this former tractation.

Solution. It is placed in all this former tractation for two causes, the one is, that it should be distinguished by that name from the other *sol*, and the other is, because it hath bene a name vsed from the beginning, and now commonly changed into *sol, euphoniæ gratia* : it may sometimes neuerthelesse be vsed, for (as I sayd before) the cunning singing man keeping euery note in his right tune, may name it according to his pleasure, for these names be no necessary accidents, for you see daylie that when any song is lettred, these names be not attributed to them, though then they be sung in their owne order, according to the opinion of many, yea very many. I know I should adde a third exception, that is to say, to except also, that euery note hauing a sharpe beefore it, should be named *mi*, as in this example,  the third note. And because that of that opinion there bee so many, I will for them shew a probable reason as by our principles may be shewed : then after by resoluing them, shewe what is most profitable, not refuting the opinion as an errour, beecause that looking to the matter, wee may finde that they may bee named as well *mi*, as *fa*, insomuch as the names (as I sayd before) are no necessary accidents, but neuerthelesse, because heere we seeke the most apt name, it were vnfit to passe it ouer. Wherefore the principall argument for them wee may in this sort forme.

Obiection. We should name all notes so neare as wee can, according as such notes are named in the *gamvt*, for it is certain, that these are the names which are most fit,

for

for so in the beginning by the first inuentors of Musick they haue bene set downe : but no note that is sharp in the *gamut* is named *fa*,therefore no note made sharp by a collaterall reason, should bee named *fa*. Secondly, throughout all the *gam vt*,from *sol* to *fa*.Next vnder it is a whole note,but from that *sol* to that *fa*, if we should call it *fa*,is but halfe a note,therefore if we call it *fa*,wee breake altogether the rule of *gamvt*,which wee should obserue : thirdly euery place in the *gam vt* that is sharp, is named either *mi* or *la*. Therefore this note (beecause not so aptly *la*)must be named *mi*.Before we fully satis-fie these arguments,one thing must necessarily be know-en : that is to say,that in naming the notes in *gam vt* the first inuentors did obserue two things, whereof the one was,to name the notes according to the *vt* : the other, to name euery note which is sharpe (as the argument proueth) *mi*, or *la* : and it falleth out sometimes,when notes flat by collaterall reasons are made sharp,that one of these two must necessarily be violated,that is to say, that eyther the note must not bee named according to the *vt*, or a note sharp must bee named *fa*, so that the controuersie lyeth in knowing, whether of these two should soonest be obserued : so according to this we answere to their arguments.To the first,where they impute a fault in vs for naming a note sharp, *fa*, seeing that no sharp note in all the *gam vt* is named *fa*,we may impute an other absurditie to them,seeing they would haue the next note vnder *sol*,*mi*,which is not found in all *gam vt*, which is the more absurditie(as we will proue in the so-lution to the third argument) To the second,the solu-

tion

tion is eafie, that euen as euery *fol* to *fa*, next vnder it is
a whole note : fo from euery *fol* to *mi*, next vnder it is
more : fo that according to the *gam vt*, in that refpect
none of them is true. To the third wee anfwere, that it
may bee as well *la*, as *mi*, becaufe that if ther were any
reafon why it fhould not be as well *la*, it might well be,
to efchew this abfurditie, that then in two places together there fhould bee one name, becaufe the next vnder
it is alfo *la*, but by naming it *mi*, the fame abfurditie
commeth in another place, therfor the one is as abfurd
as the other, as in this example, where two [music]
places together muft according to them bee named *mi*,
but to name two places together with one name, there
is none but will think more diffonant, then to name
them with diuers, whatfoeuer : for if a man did name
mi, fix times together in one place, beeing quauers, the
one comming faft vpon the other, would make them
feeme as though it were *mim, mim, mim*, as for example, [music] wherby it plainely appeareth
that this is moft abfurd. But becaufe that it were as good
that our felues fhould bring that, which others may do,
by fharp grating vpon our folutions, in this fort we may
frame a reply. Let vs fuppofe, that in the middle of a
fong which had *fa* in *C fol fa vt*, there came two notes,
one in *C fol fa vt*, & another in *B fa b mi*, hauing a flat
before it, then if the latter note in *B fa b mi*, hauing the
flat before it, be not called *fa*, it is againft the order of
the *vt*, which by the folutions fhould moft be kept, if it
be named *fa*, then commeth the abfurditie proued in the

laft

laſt example : that is, that two places together ſhould haue one name, and likewiſe if ſixe quauers did come in that ſort, the faſt comming of the one vpon the other, would make them ſeeme to be *faf, faf, faf,* which is as abſurd and diſſonant, as *mim, mim, mim.*

Reſolution. Of the flat ſo comming, and of the ſharp, there is not like reaſon, becauſe that the flat ſo comming ſhould alter the *vt,* ſo that as many notes as had come in *C ſol fa vt,* after the flat, ſhould be named *ſol,* and not *fa,* but for the firſt note, & the ſecond, they muſt be both *fa,* neuertheleſſe becauſe there may not be many of them together, as there may be of *mi,* & becauſe that in quauers, twiſe *fa,* in that ſort likely neuer chanceth, the one is not ſo abſurd as the other.

Replication. It is graunted by the laſt ſolution, that the flat ſo comming ſhould alter the *vt,* but to alter the *vt,* doth alter the key (which is in muſick a great abſurditie) therefore by the laſt ſolution, there is a great abſurditie graunted.

Solution. It is graunted conditionally, that is to ſay, if the like happened (as in the argument obiected) though ſometimes in the middeſt of a ſong, to change the key, and come into it againe, is allowed. Wherefore for the names, being the leaſt neceſſary and moſt troubleſome accident, let this ſuffice.

For *Quantitie. Cap.* 2.

There be eight quantities whereof euery one hath his proper marke, and proper reſt, as followeth.

Large

Large.
Longe.
Breefe.
Semibreefe
Minim.
Cratchet.
Quauer.
femiquauer

The proportion that thefe quantities hath one to an-other is that there fhould goe two of euery one to the next vpward as two femiquauers, to a quauer, two qua-uers to a cratchet, two cratchets to a minim, &c.

To thefe are reduced the quantities of proportions, as where there goeth three cratchets to a minim length of which the black femibreefe comprehendeth two, & ther the minim reft is but as long as one of thefe cratchets.

Heere note that the prick is in quantitie half fo long as the note before it : as a prick after a large, is in quan-titie as a long &c.

Prickes of diuifion are vfed to feperate diuerfitie of kindes in quantitie.

For Time. Cap. 3.

There be 2. kindes of time, Semibreefe time, & three

B.   minim

minim time. Semibrefe time is the ſtriking vp & downe of the hand equally in length continuing. Three minim time is the ſtriking downe & then vp of the hand equally in length, making each latter ſtroke, iuſt halfe the former.

The marke of the former kinde of time is. ¢

The marke of the latter is. ₵

In tuning Songs of Semibreefe time, you muſt put of the notes, as much as maketh a minim legth to euery mouing of the hand, likewiſe in the minim time, ſaue that to euery ſtroke there goeth but a minim length.

Heere note that theſe two kindes of time, may be deuided into minim time, by keeping all ſtrokes equall in length, putting a minim length to euery whole ſtroke.

For Tune. Cap. 4.

There be eight notes, whoſe aſcention, and deſcention doe comprehend all tunes, as the roote doth the tree, be they neuer ſo difficult, with flats and Sharps, who ſo knew how to vſe them, the notes are common, the vſe is rare, or not yet found, which being knowen, will giue great light to Muſitions, & breed great eaſe to Singing men, the eight notes are theſe that follow, as :

The tune of theſe eight Notes is to be learned by practiſe, and to be beleeued as a principle in Muſicke.

Tune the firſt Note of any ſong as it ſerueth beſt for the voyce.

If

If the Note from which and to which you goe, be both according to the Vt, of the Song, count according to the eight notes altogether.

If the note to which you goe bee altered by some intermingled flat, then for comptings sake name the Note from which you goe, as well as the note to which you goe, according to the *Vt*, of that intermingled flat, and in so doing take great care not to loose the tune of the note from which you compt, as,

First sing thus : then compt thus : and so proceede thus.

If the Note to which you goe, be altered in tune by some intermingled sharp, obserue both in the note from which and to which you goe, this Rule.
Compt to the tune of sharps by the Vt, put down to the third place, when you haue thus compting by wrong names gotten the right tunes, giue the right names after, as :

First sing thus : then compt thus : and so proceede thus .

The sharp may be put in the vpper fa, in the nether fa, and in Vt.

The sharp in the Vt, taketh place of the sharp in the vpper or nether fa, for by the Vt of it, the other two places should be sharp, the rest of the places remaining na-

turally

turally : as,

Vt for compting.

Likewise the sharp in the nether fa, taketh place of the sharp in the vpper fa, for by the Vt of the ✂ in the nether fa, the vpper fa must bee sharp, the rest remaining naturally : as,

Vt for Compting.

The flat may be put in two places, in Mi, and in La, also it is common in Mi, but not so common in La: also if the flat be in La (according to the Vt of it) Mi must be flat : as,

Heere note that for to tune sharps, put downe Vt, to the third place.

If the note to which you goe may neither in tuning nor naming belong to one order of ascention, go back to the note before, and so Compt : as,

sol   fa   fa   mi   sol   fa

First begin thus, Then go back thus, and so proceed thus.

As

As men name according to the *Vt*, of the flat, so there be, that (for facility & fitneſſe of the name to the tune) do name according to the *Vt* of the ſharp ſomtimes: as,

mi re mi.

Heere note, that the intermingled flat beareth force but whileſt notes as appendant come in the ſame place, though for handſomneſſe men name beefore or after according to it :   Likewiſe the ſharp, as,

la

Thappendancy of the flat by the ſharp, and of the ſharp by the Flat is taken away, though by negligence and ignorance of prickers, we are oft driuen to gather thappendancie by the courſe of the ſong. Looke in the laſt example.

The prick is to be continued and kept in one tune with the note before it.

Heere note, that the Cleues may remoue from one rule to another, and that they are vſed for Flats. Alſo that the Direct is put to ſhew the note following : as,

Euery Note in the order of Aſcenſſion is a whole

note

note or tone aboue the next vnder, saue the vpper & nether Fa, which be but halfe notes or Semitones.

For redinesse in setting Notes distant, let the learner
practise these examples following, with all such things
as make varietie in naming, or tuning.

Also for readines, note that euery foure rules & a space
further, maketh an eight, & euery eight, hath like names.

vt mi re fa mi sol fa la la fa sol mi fa re mi vt re vt

sol fa la sol mi la fa fa sol sol sol fa fa la mi sol re fa sol

sol la sol fa sol sol sol la sol mi sol fa sol sol sol la sol fa sol sol sol.

Sol la fa sol la la mi fa fa fa sol la fa sol la fa sol sol fa mi fa fa la sol sol la sol.

Rules of Song.

Fa sol fa la fa sol fa la la mi fa sol fa sol la fa fa fa la sol fa.

O God that art my righteousnesse, Lord heare me vvhen I call,

thou hast set mee at libertie, vvhen I vvas bound and thral.

The 3 parts
follovv.

The Church Tune.

Fa la mi fa sol fa sol fa fa fa la mi la sol la la la sol sol sol mi fa sol fa.

Fa la sol la sol fa sol la mi fa sol fa fa la la sol la fa la sol fa fa la la sol fa.

B.iij   The

The post rules of Song.

Heere followeth the post rules of Song, which are reduced to the vnlimited obseruations vsed in Singing.

For naming. Cap. I.

He exceptions from the order of ascention & descention are diuersely vsed according to the diuersitie of place, and accordingly, they are to bee giuen, for each order in naming seemeth best to them that haue beene brought vp withall.

D, is sometimes vsed in old songs as a Cleue, and putteth Vt downe to the fift place.

In Italy (as I vnderstand) they change Vt into Sol : In England they change Re, into La : when the next remouing Note before or after be vnder.

Some there bee that vse sometimes in defending at this day, the names of Re, and Vt, there be that name at randon, some for pleasure, and some through ignorant imagination, often times beareth great force in making a thing seeme comely, or vncomely, as if in comming downe, Sol, Fa, La, Sol, a man should name the first two notes Re Mi, it would seeme to a singing man very vncomely : yet if the singing man did imagin, that the finger were putting a ditie, or word of foure sillables,

as :

as : Remigrare, to these foure Notes, he would not think
it vncomely, & yet in doing the deed, both waies are all
one, for the first two sillables of, Remigrare, are Re, Mi.

For Quantitie. Cap. II.

TO make one and the selfe same mark of quantitie
sometimes long, and sometimes short, Musitions in
old time, borrowed colours of the Painters, sometimes
making it red, and sometimes black, &c.

They borrowed numbers of Arithmatike, sometimes
making this, and sometimes that figure, &c.

They borrowed Circles and Semicircles of Geome-
trie, sometimes putting in the Center or a lyne, & sometimes leauing it out, &c. Sometimes also thereby signi-
fying alteration in time.

They borrowed similitudes of Philosophie, sometimes leauing fulnesse, and sometimes Eclips, as appeareth in the Moone, sometimes knitting and sometimes
loosing, as in generation and corruption.

They vsed moreouer many signes and tokens and
marks of Quantitie, that are cut off as superfluous.

They vsed also manifold names to distinguish these
things one from another, to the wonderfull pestering of
the memory, & great toile of the vnderstanding, though
some of them wer necessary, yet many were superflous.

The Quantities in Proportion are diuers, according
to the diuersitie of Proportions, which are *infinite in po-
tentia*, that is to say; in possibilitie of increase, as nūber is.

Many of these things are yet vsed, as the Semibreefe

rest,

reft, in three minim time, for three minim refts.

Some ftrange markes and knitting of Notes which time I doubt not will cut off, neuerthelefſe heere ſhall follow examples of ſome, to which the redſidue are to be reduced.

Perfect moode.   Perfect moode.   Imperfect moode.   perfect time.

Imperfect time.   Maior prolation.   Minor prolation.

O³· O₂· C₃· C₂· ⊙ · ₵ · φ · ₵

Perfect moode, perfect time.

Perfect moode, Imperfect time.

Imperfect moode, perfect time.

Imperfect moode, Imperfect time.

Prolation Maior, perfect time.

Prolation Minor, Imperfect time.

Diminution, perfect time.

Diminution, Imperfect time.

By

Rules of Song.

By these examples following, the foure Modes are knowne what quātitie the lesser notes are to the greater.

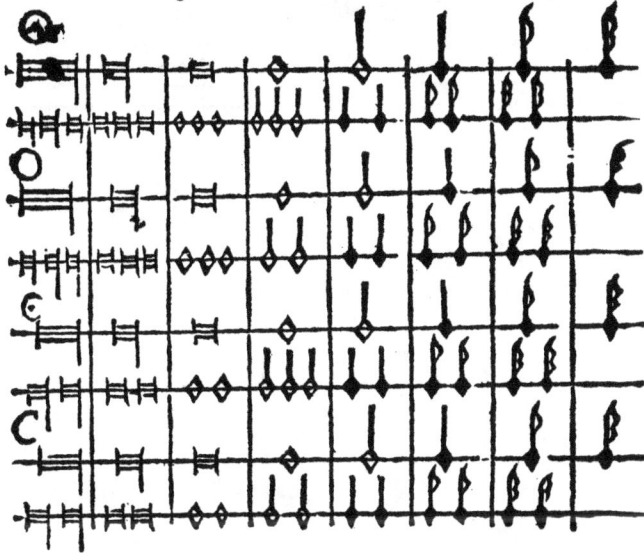

The lovver notes are as much in quantitie as the higher vvith their pricks.

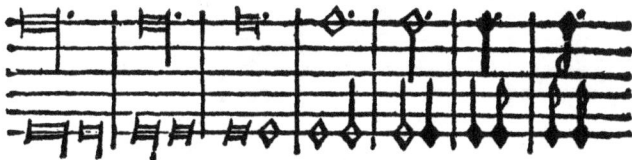

Pricks of Diuision are those, vvhich are set aboue notes and not by them, and they shevv the note to bee perfect before the prick : and the note follovving doth belong to another ſtroke.

a longa

Rules of Song.

a longs to the blacke large.　　a briefes to the black long,　　2 semibreefes to the black briefe.　　2 minims to the black semibrief.

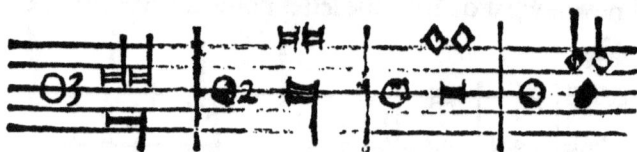

XII Examples of Legatures.

More Examples of Legatures, as followeth.

For Time. Cap.III.

IN timing hard proportions that go odding, many take care onely of the whole stroke, wholy kept without deuiding it to the going vp & then downe agayne of the hand.

Some keepe Semibreefe time, as sufficient easie of it selfe, and doe not diuide it into minim time.

Three minim time is more difficult, and therefore some doe diuide it into minim time: as,

Take a stick of a certaine length, and a stone of a certaine weight, hold the stick standing vpon an end of some

some table: See you haue vpon the stick diuers marks: hold the stone vp by the side of the stick : then as you let fall the stone, instantly begin to sing one Note, and iust with the noyse that it maketh vpon the table, beegin another Note, and as long as thou holdest the first Note, so long hold the rest, and let that note thy Cratchet or thy Minim, &c. as thou seest cause, and thus maist thou measure the very Time it selfe that thou keepest, and know whether thou hast altered it, or not.

For Tune . Cap.IIII.

Ome learne to Tune only by the Voice of anoher : some vse helpe of an Instrument, which is the better way.

Learners vse to tune by a certaine continuance of time, according to the *Vt* of the song, before they practise intermingled Flats or sharps.

Heere note, that C. called Csolfavt cleue, is a fift beneth G. called Gsolrevt cleue, and F. called Ffavt cleue, is a fift beneth C. called Csolfavt, Cleue.

Also a man may compt from any cleue, by the letters, compting them forward when hee goeth vpward, and acompting them backward when he goeth downward, telling but the first seuen letters : by the knowledge of this, men may giue their tunes to the parts without knowledge of the Gamvt. Yet for the common vse, it were not amisse, that learners should sometime or other commit the Gam-vt to memory.

Many things are heere taught by rule, for which
teachers

teachers heeretofore, gaue no rule, and if they were af-
ked how fhall a man know the like? they would anfwere, that is according to the courfe of the Song, but
this anfwere is fo vncertaine, that it is as good for the
yong Scoller, they had faid we know not.

¶ A generall Table comprehending two parts in one,
of all kindes vpon all plaine Songs, vpon all pricke
Songs, and in all wayes that may be found, one part
beginning, th'other following, the plaine Song or
ground being fung beneth them: all which are found
by this prefent table, with fuch facilitie, that the
vpper part is made, and neuer booked, as heere followeth.

The

The obser uations of the places vp are sixe	85	11	10	9	8	7	6
6	85	11	10	9	8	7	6
5	1	7	6	5	4	3	2
4	7	6	5	4	3	2	1
3	2	1	7	6	5	4	3
2	5	6	7	1	2	3	4
1	1	2	3	4	5	6	7
Places vp.	1	7	6	5	4	3	2

Courses vp	Courses downe							
1		1356	6	135	16	35	136	5
2	7	6	135	16	35	136	5	1356
3	6	135	16	35	136	5	1356	6
4	5	16	35	136	5	1356	6	135
5	4	35	136	5	1356	6	135	36
6	3	136	5	1356	6	135	16	35
7	2	5	1356	6	135	16	35	136
8 vt su: 1		1356	6	135	16	35	136	5
Places down		1	2	3	4	5	6	7

The obser uations of the places down are sixe							
1	1	2	3	4	5	6	7
2	5	6	7	1	2	3	4
3	2	3	4	5	6	7	1
4	7	1	2	3	4	5	6
5	1	2	3	4	5	6	7
6	5	6	7	8	9	10	11

Thus

His prefent table, may ferue alfo, who fo marketh it well, for 2 parts in one, without a plaine fong, of all kinds, & in all waies for 3 parts in one, without a plainfong, or ground, the third part being vnder : of all kindes & of all wayes for 2 parts in one, vpon 2 plain fongs, or grouds at once, for maintaining reports, & other fuch things as thefe be.

Firft it is to be vnderftanded by this word place, is ment the diftance of the following part, to the former part, as the fame place or vnifon, is called the firft place, the next or fecond place is called the fecond place, whether it be vp or downe, &c.

Next heere is to be vnderftanded that by this word, Courfe, is ment the diftaunce of that which followeth iuft fo long after, as the following part refteth to that which goeth beefore, in the plaine Song or ground, as if the following part haue a Semibreefe reft, then the Note of tbe ground is in the firft courfe, which hath in the fame place that which followeth, iuft a Semibreefe length after, and that note is in the fecond courfe, which hath in the fecond place that which followeth iuft a Semibreefe length after, whether it bee vp or downe, &c.

Thus beeing knowne, firft looke in what place vp or downe, you would haue the following part to bee, which is according to the pleafure of the maker, and fo it is how long the following part fhall reft. Then looke in what courfe vp or downe is the note of the ground, for which you would make, then looke what fquare of the table meeteth with the place and courfe, and there

C.   you

you shall finde noted by figures, what concord serueth for that course.

All Concords next expressed in the square, make discords betwixt the vpper part and the plaine song or ground. Neuerthelesse, they may be brought in, when they may be garded by the place next adioyning, for whatsoeuer maketh a discord, the next place to it maketh a concord.

Note also that iust so long before the close, as the following part resteth, you make not that which breedeth a discord, betwixt the vpper part and the ground, nor that which to the close of the ground is one more in number then the second figure of obseruation.

Note also, that if iust so long before the close as the following part resteth, you make that which to the close is two more in number then the first figure of obseruation, then the best way is to make it sharp.

Note also, that from the beginning forth, of so farre before the close, as the following part resteth, all concords serueth.

The exposition of the figure
of obseruation.

He first and second figures sheweth what distaunces (in respect of the latter notes of the course) should not come twise together, remouing one way with the latter notes, and also where in respect of the latter note of the course, a
flat

flat for a sharp,or a sharp for a flat, contrary to the order of the place should not bee.

The third & fourth sheweth what mouing one way with the place, iust so long after as the following part resteth,maketh discords.

The fift and sixt serueth wherein the distance, there should not be like mouing one way with the place iust so long after as the following part resteth,and the fift figure; Also where sharp for flat,or flat for sharp,contrary to the order of the place should not bee iust so long after as the following resteth.

Heere note,that vnder each number are comprehended all those that maketh eights,or concords,of that kinde to it,except that vnder the last figure of obseruation such as make eights to the number one way with the place,and such as make ninthes to it in the contrary way are comprehended.

Heere note that two parts in one in the vnizon, fourth, and fift, doe differ from the rest,for in the rest, both parts are tyed,to like order of ascention,but in these both parts do keepe like order according to their place.

Note also, that in two parts in one,in the fourth vp, and in the fift downe, the vpper fa, kept flat in the nether parts causeth a strange flat to be brought in the vpper part,therefore the best way is to make it sharp,vnlesse it bee in such places as a strange flat will doe well to come in.

Two verses comprehending the foresaid Table,
which for necessities sake of the matter, must
be written crossing one another

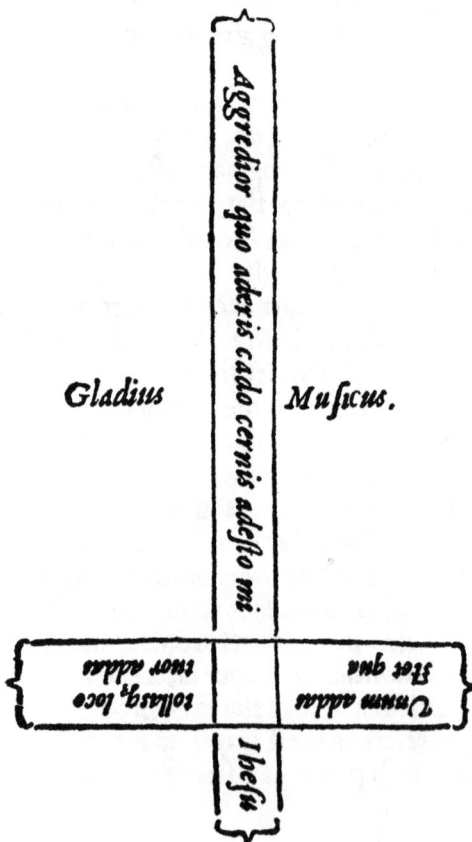

Aggredior quo aderis cado cernis adesto mi

Gladius   Musicus.

Unum addas
stet qua

rollasq́, loce
tuor addas

Ibesis

In

Rules of Song.

IN this Table or figure aforesayde, foure things are comprehended, the places, the 6. figures of obseruation belonging to them, the courses and concords ser-uing for them, for the seuen places, there be seuen words in the blade of the Sword : the first word, *Aggredior*, is alwaies for the first place : the second word downward, *quo*, is for the second place downeward, &c. And the second word vpward, *mi*, is for the second place vpward, &c. This word, *Ihesu*, is cut off from the rest, to signifie that it beelongeth to another kinde, for in it the letters numerable being 5. doe signifie the first and second fi-gures of obseruation, and it is written one way with the verse, to signifie that it goeth according to the woord of the verse, which is for the place, for it signifieth one number with the word of the verse, that standeth for the place, as if the word bee the fourth word of the verse, then it signifieth, 4. &c. and 5. signifieth the fift num-ber, to that, as the fift number to foure is 8. and so are the first and second figures of obseruation found. Then are the other foure figures of obseruation to bee found by the crosse verse, which sayth : adde one to the place, take one from the place, let the pl.... st.and, adde foure to the place, and so shall you finde the third, fourth, fift, and sixt figures of obseruation.

Heere note, that if the place be the vnizon, beecause you cannot take one from a vnizon, take it from eight, which is of the same kinde, when you haue thus done, tourne the poynt of the Sword downe, and then the se-uen woords, serueth for the seuen courses in this order : First the word that serueth for the place, serueth for the

first

Rules of Song.

firſt courſe, the ſecond woord vpward, for the ſecond
courſe vpward : the ſecond woord downeward, for the
ſecond courſe downward, &c. As the Sword now ſtandeth, compting about vpon the ſeuen words, when you
haue found what woord ſerueth for the courſe, looke
what vowels bee in it, and thereby you ſhall know the
concords, that ſerueth for that courſe, as if the vowell
bee A, it ſignifieth the vnizon. If it be E, it ſignifieth the
third. If it bee I, it ſignifieth the fift. And if it be O, it
ſignifieth the ſixt. Lo, thus are all the things expreſſed at
large in the table, briefely contriued in the compaſſe of
two verſes.

The

Rules of Song.

The names of the Cords for Counterpoint, Defcant, and any fet Song in how many parts foeuer.

A concord is diuided into an { Vnizon. Third.. Fift. Sixt. Eight. Tenth. Twelfth. Thirtenth. & a Fiftenth }

Difcord are thefe. { A fecond. A fourth. A feuenth. A Ninth. A leuenth. A foureteth. } & their eights.

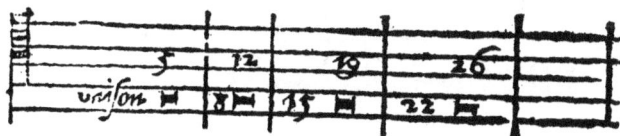

Concords, perfect and vnperfect.

Concords, perfect and vnperfect.

Rules of Song.

Discords.

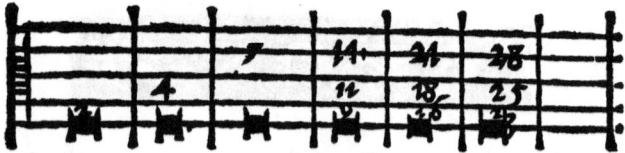

Concords.

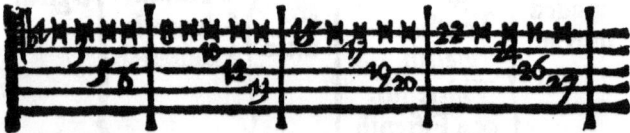

De

Rules of Song.

De Inuentione.

CRefcit in infinitum, Inuentio tempore cuncto,
Sed tribus eft dixis fape morata malis.

Eft mora paupertas prohibens Inuenta probari,
Non poterit fieri ftultus inanis ait.

Vis, piger inquit, adire via latitante leone?
Sic mora pauperies, ftultus, homoq, piger.

Laus nunc, laus femper, laus omni tempore fummo:
Difcens atq, docens, dicite: lausq, Deo.

FINIS.

CANTVS.

G.K.

O Lord in thee is all my trust, giue eare vnto my wofull cry:

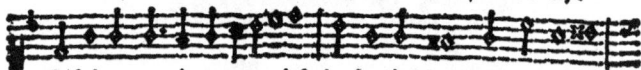

Refuse mee not that am vn— iust, but bovving dovvne thy heauenly eie.

Behold hovv I doe still lament, my sinnes vvherein I doe offend:

O Lord for them shall I bee shent, sith thee to pleafe I doe entend.

TENOR.

O Lord in thee: &c.

ALTUS. G.K.

O Lord in thee, &c.

BASSUS.

O Lord in thee, &c.

10. fundry waies of 2. parts in one vpon the plain fong.

1.

2.

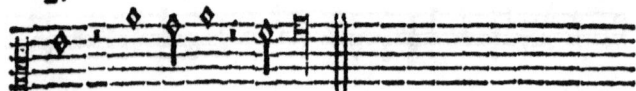

3.

4.

10. fundry waies of 2 parts in one vpon the plain fong.

5.

6.

10. sundry waies of 2 parts in one vpon the plain song.

7.

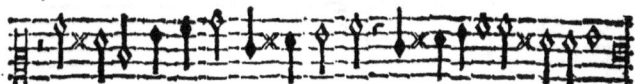

8.

9.

10.

FINIS. Place the Table of the comparisons of Cliffes after this.